Freedom Pearls Around the Table

Shaila Kerr

To all women everywhere who wish to find "Freedom Pearls"; especially the three women I pray for the most: my future daughters-in-law. You were born to shift atmospheres & you will change the world!

Table of Contents

Letter to Freedom Pearls..4
Introduction..6
The Basics..7
Freedom Pearls: Meeting One...14
Freedom Pearls: Meeting Two...25
Freedom Pearls: Meeting Three..34
Freedom Pearls: Meeting Four..42
Freedom Pearls: Meeting Five – "No Masks"...............................52
Final Thoughts..62
Recipes..63
Administrative Documents...70
Testimonials..72
Acknowledgments..75
Author Biography...77

Letter to Freedom Pearls

Before we start…I bless your Spirit to *closely connect* with ABBA.

Take a few seconds to really allow this blessing to sink in. *Breathe deeply*.

Trust and know wholeheartedly that you will lack absolutely nothing as you say "Yes" to mothering during these five weeks of Freedom Pearls.

Remember: You will lack nothing.

I declare over you:

You will have more than enough…

…More than enough money for what you need.

…More than enough creativity and skill.

…More than enough gifting and supernatural ability to teach, release, and empower.

I release over you a special grace to mentor women into being comfortable with Love in such a way that they attract Love and find true Freedom.

I bless the leader in you to deliver this message of Love and Freedom, all the while being the object of His affections as He uses YOU—the incredible, brave YOU—for His Glory and to Love other sisters well.

I bless you with supernatural hospitality, the ability to "enlarge and stretch up", just like in Isaiah 54, for you will no longer live in shame.

> *"Enlarge your house; build an addition. Spread out your home, and spare no expense! 3 For you will soon be bursting at the seams. Your descendants will occupy other nations and resettle the ruined cities. 4 "Fear not; you will no longer live in shame. Don't be afraid; there is no more disgrace for you. You will no longer remember the shame of your youth and the sorrows of widowhood. 5 For your Creator will be your husband; the LORD of Heaven's Armies is his name! He is your Redeemer, the Holy One of Israel, the God of all the earth. 6 For the LORD has called you back from your grief— as though you were a young wife abandoned by her husband," says your God.*
> *--Isaiah 54:2-6 NLT--*

Are you ready?

*Throughout the book, any time you see asterisks around a sentence, **stop** and take three to five deep breaths as you ponder, responding to Holy Spirit*

Any time you see text in purple, it signifies that the author, Shaila, is speaking directly to you.

He delights in you.

Introduction

The name says it all. It's Freedom Pearls Around the Table, so as we serve a meal and provide communion and community by intentionally taking time to do so, we trust that Holy Spirit will do the rest (…and He totally does!).

So, what is Freedom Pearls Around the Table? I'm glad you asked! It is:

> **…5 Saturdays…**
> **…for 5 hours…**
> **…away from everyone and everything besides our group of ladies…**
> **…committed (all of us will have to lock in those five Saturdays for five hours)…**
> **…and intentionally pursuing relationship with each other and with ABBA.**

The goal of these meetings is to help you grow, heal, and find your purpose as the Beloved in the heart of ABBA. Each week, you will help the women that surround you into a deeper revelation of what it means to be "made whole" by the love of ABBA! So many women are walking around broken and hurting, struggling in their relationship with the Lord, their spouse, their family, etc. And they've never understood the gifts of community and wholeness. They've never found the joy that comes from God changing their life and teaching them who they really are in Him!

The Bible says that when we press in and seek ABBA and his healing love, we will be filled and made whole (Jeremiah 29:13, Colossians 2:9-10). Freedom Pearls agrees with God's Word and helps each woman break free of the pain and negativity that has held them back! What can you expect as we pursue ABBA's Freedom Pearls Around the Table?

- **Answered Questions as you awaken areas of your heart that were numb**
- **Dreams and Goals (not the ones that you learn in coaching)**
- **Embracing Godly Grieving (it has a beginning, middle and an end)**
- **Embracing Pain as part of the journey**
- **Experiencing and Releasing Forgiveness and Supernatural Breakthroughs**
- **Healing from Abuse [Sexual, Physical, and Emotional]**
- **More of the Holy Spirit and the Prophetic**
- **Prosperity of the Soul**
- **Joyfully Enjoying the Process**
- **Understanding your Influence as you "Queen Up"**
- **Learning a bit more about Prophecy and Personalities in the Prophetic**

Get ready; this will be a 5-week journey that will change both your life and those that choose to join you!

The Basics

What this Manual Includes

This manual provides the basics for completing Freedom Pearls Around the Table – the framework of the canvas, if you will. However, it's up to **you** to fill it with color! My goal is to help you along the way, provide wisdom (what to do and what *not* to do), and build a structure for community, fellowship, and healing in your community!

Following this section which introduces the basics of what you will do and what you need, there is an in-depth explanation for each of the five meetings. Each day includes a menu (detailed recipes are at the back of the book!), what you will need for that day, a schedule, and instructions on how to execute each activity. {Remember, the schedule is an aid, but DON'T turn it into legalism and feel pressured to stick to it without fail; the Spirit is the best guide!}

My first tip for you is this: if your group of women grows to be five or larger (including yourself), break them up into small groups of three. This will help some of the exercises flow much more quickly and smoothly and will encourage them to go deep with the women in their small group.

What You Will Do

Each week, we will pursue the heart of ABBA toward his beloved daughters, pushing closer to his purpose and desires for each of the women in your group. We will do this in a couple different ways, including:

1. **Freedom Pearls -** These are the core of Freedom Pearls Around the Table. They are tried and tested methods that dig deep into the hearts, souls, and spirits of each woman, erasing lack and filling each one with the love of ABBA. Be prepared for some of the deepest and most wonderful moments of your five weeks to happen here!
    a. When we did our Freedom Pearls, I actually went to Michael's and bought a bag of "pearls". Every time we finished a Freedom Pearls section, I gave each woman a pearl to take home. It was a nice touch and I highly recommend it!
2. **Exercises** – These are quicker, often more mental exercises that will help the women process what the Lord is saying to them or prepare them for the next section.
3. **Meals** – Meals are some of the most important connection and community times we can have! They feature prominently in both Jesus' ministry and the Early Church of Acts and we have found that some of the best times are found around the dinner table together! Sharing a meal together is also where we get to know each other well, look into each other's eyes, and connect in an intentional way.

4. **Readings** – Often, there will be readings out of the Bible or a few other resources as we dive into the love and words of ABBA through His Spirit!
5. **Much More!** – Be prepared for a myriad of different experiences as you lead your group to experience God's love and find freedom pearls around the table!

What You'll Need Every Week

Creating the Atmosphere:
- Your favorite scented candles: Lots of them! {And ask Holy Spirit what to pick every week.}
- Different Decorative Themes for each week
    - No detail is too small! Pray about everything: from your flowers to your napkins, and even your paper goods. Everything will release a prophetic reality into the room.
- Journals
    - Ask Holy Spirit which journals to select for your group and why. {You will share this with the women.} Don't worry; He *will* show you!
    - Each woman will have to bring back their journals weekly.
- Colored pens and pencils available for notetaking and art
- Flower arrangements
    - They can be simple. They can be hand-picked or store bought. The point is: *keep them fresh and beautiful*. {Have one at every table, bathroom, and meeting room.}
- Tablecloths {They should be cloth, not paper or plastic. Vary them weekly, if possible.}
- If weather permits, use the outdoors: Set your tables in nature (backyards, patios, under trees etc.)
    - Feel free to use creation for inspiration!
- Chairs for everyone {And comfy, cute pillows.}
- A Contribution Tin!

For the Table
- A nice beverage corner: Water, Fruit-infused water, Coffee and creamers, and a different juice every time.
- The serving table: Nice tablecloth, serving utensils, and support for hot dishes
    - {Don't forget the flowers and candles!}
- An available sound system {preferably Bluetooth-enabled so that it can easily connect to your cellphone}
- Table(s) set for eating for all
    - Everyone should have a seat with their name on it. Swap where they sit weekly.
- Placement name tags or cards for the dinner table seating arrangement {You can make them yourself or buy them.}

Freedom Pearls Around the Table Shaila Kerr

- Your own dishes for the meal and dessert or you can play around with different disposable dishes weekly {Once again: Ask Holy Spirit! Be creative and choose pretty, girly things.}
- Your meals: The food is important. We must serve something nice and delicious, however, at no point in time is the menu to be a reason for anxiety. Joy is the key ingredient! If you need to, it's better for you to serve pizza and salad, hotdogs, or cheese platters—but put it together with great joy! Serve with the heart of the King; rule with the heart of a servant!

Resources:
- Your Bible
- Hinds' Feet on High Places: Delightfully Illustrated and Arranged for Children by Hannah Hurnard
- Blessing Your Spirit by Arthur Burk and Sylvia Gunter
- Be creative! {You can't get this wrong. *Let the Holy Spirit lead!*}
- Have Fun!

The Contribution Tin

As you plan your meals, buy your books, and prepare your different table settings and candles, remember that these things every week do add up. Since Freedom Pearls for five weeks does not have a predetermined cost and we are not charging the women to attend, we would like to teach each Pearl the importance of generosity. Radical generosity is one of the necessary signs of culture transformation and revival. As you prepare for the meetings, separate a cute container (It can be a tin, a box, a basket, etc. - But make it pretty!) and write a sign on it that reads: "Donations for this week's Freedom Pearls Session Here."

On your first session explain a little bit about it. The contribution/generosity tin is to encourage the women to give. Each woman should be propelled to give at least enough to cover their dinner, dessert, and coffee/tea weekly (around $20), however, some women may not be able to do so. Some will be able to contribute with more; encourage them to do so, as they could cover for some women who might be in a tight place financially! Wherever they may be, they are invited into the blessing of making Freedom Pearls Around the Table possible for all.

Remember! Don't get discouraged or grow weary if people don't contribute with a lot. God will back it up. Your faith will be stretched and you can always review your menu and cut back in some costs a bit, but the spirit is of excellence and beauty, to reflect HIS KINGDOM! Be creative! For some of you, you could set your table in your beautiful backyard, and nature can be your decor... (weather allowing). For others, you can pick fresh flowers and save a few bucks from having to buy them and you could use your own dishes instead of anything disposable and make it really pretty.

At the end of the day, the idea is: **Don't let money be the reason you don't do your five weeks!** God will bring in all that you need. You can test Him on it: He did it for me, He can do it again! Restoring these women through these five weeks for five hours is first His heart, community around the table is Jesus' model (the whole book of Acts resembles that) and God will give you the grace and all you need!

And on that encouraging note, let us begin!

Notes

Notes

Notes

Freedom Pearls: Meeting One

Menu Suggestion

- Arugula Salad with parmesan cheese and lime vinaigrette
- Artichoke & Spinach risotto
- Marinated, pan-fried, sliced Chicken Breast (place chicken on top of each risotto dish)
- Sparkling Water & Cranberry punch
- Grapes & Strawberries {YUM!}

What You'll Need

- Pastel Colored Cardstock {It can just be white sheets of paper if that's all you can get, too}
- Washable Markers (1 per person)
- Tape
- Bluetooth Speaker {If you're anything like me, you might want to check ahead of time to make sure that it is already in sync with your phone. Tech stuff can be hard!}

{Today is ALL about allowing the Holy Spirit and ABBA to speak identity over the Freedom Pearls. Therefore, due to the nature of our exercises for this gathering, DO NOT provide nametags (besides the ones on the table at dinner), formal introductions, or anything that puts a name and identity to the women, in any way. Trust me, this is very important!}

Schedule

- Welcome [15 minutes]
- Share the Vision [15 minutes]
- Exercise One: Romantic Song [12 minutes]
- Ice-Breaker [30 minutes]
- Dinner, Dessert, & Table Talks [1 hour & 30 minutes]
- Bathroom Break [10 minutes]
- Exercise Two: Intentional Forgiveness [50 minutes]
- Response & Forgiveness Pearl [1 hour & 10 minutes]

Welcome Words & Announcements [15 min]

Take this time as you are greeting the women to share necessary information such as parking, restrooms, etc. Share with them the process that God took you through to select them, make sure they feel and know that they were specially chosen, hand-picked (just like a pearl) to go on this journey.

Share the Vision [15 min]

Revisit and read aloud the "Letter to Freedom Pearls" (see page 1) to the women. I encourage you to also add what Holy Spirit gave you as vision for this specific group.

Exercise One [12 min]: Romantic Song

Before the meeting, make sure to have *"Wonderful Tonight (Duet with Ivan Lins)" by Michael Bublé* cued on your Bluetooth speaker.

Have the women go to their place at the table, find their name, grab the journals you bought for them, and come sit comfortably in the sitting area. The sitting area should be a Couch, Family Room, Living Room, or somewhere that you've made cozy and peacefully inviting.

Before you play the song, lead the women through this relaxation exercise, asking them to do the following:

- Close your eyes and take a few deep breaths
- *Relax* your shoulders and uncross your legs
- Take one more deep breath

In a very calm tone, guide them through this question by having them repeat after you: *"God, what do you have to say to me about how you see me? About your love for me?"*

Begin playing *Wonderful Tonight* and lead the women to just breathe, relax, and hear God's answers as the music plays.

When the song comes to an end, repeat the song again, with the same exact exercise, but this time encourage the women to write the answers God gives them in their journals.

After that, transition the women to stand up. ("We are going to start a game!")

Break the Ice [30 min]

Before the meeting, prepare as many sheets of paper as you have women in your group (including yourself). Each sheet should have vertical numbers that go up to one less than how many women are in your group. For example, if you have five ladies in your group (including yourself), you will prepare 5 papers, each numbered 1 to 4. Got it??

After announcing the game, give one sheet to each woman. {Pink is always fun but use this as another opportunity to ask the Holy Spirit to guide you in your choice.}

Say: "Have a friend tape the sheet of paper to your back for you."

After the sheets are taped to their back, have each woman choose a marker.

Ask the women to go around the room to each paper and write prophetic words or short phrases that describe the woman who has the sheet on her back.

If your group is not familiar with the prophetic, here is some guidance on how to easily introduce it:

- Briefly explain prophetic words (verses such as 1 Corinthians 14:1-5 are good to use). "As you write on a woman's back, we are stirring the belief and expectation of their greatness. Prophetic words should be wonderful, encouraging, full of Life, calling out the things that are not as if they were. An example of this would be that, if you see someone who looks depressed or profoundly sad, a prophetic word for them should say the opposite: "I see joy over your life and a shift that will uplift you and make you feel like Father God cares for and loves you". God isn't depressed and His identity is always changing his children for the better, so declare what is not as though it is!

By the end, each woman should have at least one word or phrase written from every person in the group (besides themselves of course) on their sheet of paper. When that's done, you're finished with the game!

Say: "Have a friend gently remove the paper from your back and take a seat again."

Now, it is time to share! Because your group of women have not shared anything yet, you go first! (Leaders always model what their followers will do.) Here is how to conduct the sharing time:

- Say: "I am..." and read the words given to you on the paper that was behind your back.
- *When you finish speaking out the last word, say "I am [your name]."*
- Now that you've modeled how to share, go around the room, listening to the women share words that define them and then their name, going one at a time.

It's very important that we follow two rules for sharing for every Freedom Pearls meeting:

1. Always remember that we are cultivating a safe place. So, confidentiality is essential throughout all five weeks. The ladies should feel protected when they share. Some may share things they've never told anyone about before.
2. When someone is sharing, do your best to have EVERYONE listening and preferably looking at them. You should encourage sensitivity among your group for any extra needs. (For example: gently passing a tissue, putting your hands on their shoulder or stopping for a little cold water or even a hug, depending on how much emotion is surfacing.)

You should be done with this Ice Breaker and the sharing time in 30 minutes, but make sure each woman has enough time. {Relationship over structure any day!}

Have each woman grab her journal and bring it with them to the table, because it's dinner time!

At the back of this booklet, there is a Contact Sheet. Use this sheet to collect each woman's name, number, email, and social media information. If you have a group that is large enough to require breaking down into multiple small groups, make sure each small group facilitator gets a copy of the form to collect their individual small group members' information.

There also is a Video/Photo Release Agreement in case you would like to use any photos or video taken during your current home group to advertise for any others you may choose to begin.

Dinner & Dessert [1 hour & 30 min]

Before you transition to the dining room table, give any announcements regarding the flow of dinner and a thanksgiving prayer for the food and fellowship. In addition, use this time to collect the information on the sheet above.

Once everyone is served, guide the women into a dinner table exercise:

Table Talks [during dinner]

Grab your journal and share with all of the women what the Lord said to you during the romantic song, soaking time. Each woman should be listening whole-heartedly and eating quietly. Then, go around the table and have each woman share the same.

After each woman reads what the Lord said to them, have others gather around them, pray in agreement with what God said over them, and prophesy. {This is an extremely powerful moment. Encourage ALL of the women at the table to stand in agreement, praying and prophesying. *This should not be a time just for the host! The more agreement, the more power*.}

Assign a woman to take down notes of everything that is said in each Freedom Pearl's journal while the others are praying and prophesying over her. This way, when the time is up, her journal can be given back to her with notes of what everyone said. When it is the Note-Taker's turn, swap with someone else so that notes are taken in her journal as the others prophesy and pray over her.

Quick Bathroom Break [10 min]

As a host, take this time to take the food back to the kitchen and clear the dining table from dishes. Run a fresh pot of coffee or tea and refresh or refill the water dispenser.

After the break, head back to the comfy room. Make sure to have everyone bring their journals with them.

Exercise Two: Intentional Forgiveness [50 min]

> *"And forgive us our debts, as we have forgiven our debtors [letting go of both the wrong and the resentment.]"*
> **--Matthew 6:12 AMP--**

Before this exercise: Prepare *"Letting It Die"* by Justin Byrne (Song #10 from his album *The Rest of Life*) and play it softly on repeat.

Make sure to play it at a volume that allows a little bit of privacy but doesn't drown out your voice as you dictate the exercise. Later on, when the women are writing and you aren't speaking, make it a little louder.

As the song begins playing and the women settle back down in the comfy room, prompt the group back into soaking mode. This might take a while, because women LOVE to talk. Have a kind but firm tone and reel everyone back in.

Emphasize the importance of getting started again. You are about to see Holy Spirit do the most amazing work. Just partner with His Love and keep going, don't EVER second-guess yourself. Stay vigilant against the Enemy! He's sneaky and might try to bring unbelief, discouragement, and even make you feel unqualified. Don't buy it: you are incredible! And Jesus has your back! You need nothing else.

Instruct the ladies to write this question down along with the answers the Holy Spirit gives them.

Say: "Ask Holy Spirit; 'Is there anyone in a leadership or influential role in my life that I need to forgive?'" (It can be a pastor, a boss, a spouse, a parent…)

Say this with a tranquil voice: "Take your time. Don't rush through this process, allow God to speak to you. Don't run away from going deep. Stay intentional, even when it gets intense."

Give them time to listen and write.

Say: "Now ask, 'Holy Spirit, what am I forgiving this person for? In other words, what pains have they caused me? How have they hurt me?'"

Pause, then say: "Write down everything God gives you."

Give them about **30 minutes** to complete this portion. In this same atmosphere, go to your next questions. Remind them to write them down.

Dictate the exercise SLOWLY.

Have them repeat after you: "Holy Spirit, I allow you to take me through the pains and the fears that I have felt from this person/these people and in this season/these seasons."

Wait.

Have them repeat after you: "Holy Spirit, tenderize my heart. Take me to and through any and all areas that I have blocked out, in order to survive or stay numb to pain."

Don't rush this, allow the pain to surface. Give the women about **20 minutes** to allow Holy Spirit to move within them.

Turn down the volume to keep it as ambiance music.

Response & Forgiveness Pearl [1 hour, 10 min]

On the same album, change the song to *"Then It Became Clear"* (Song #8 on the album). Make sure it is on repeat.

Now, go around the room, openly sharing everything the Lord has led each woman through. Have tissues handy and encourage other women to stand close and be kind. This exercise gets very emotional, so don't rush this process. Afterwards, have each woman pray and prophesy over the woman who just shared and unpacked part of her pain. {We suggest recording on the phones what gets prayed and prophesied over them throughout this process.}

As mentioned in the Introduction, along this 5-week journey, you will be collecting "Freedom Pearls". These are prayers led by the Holy Spirit that bring healing and fulfillment when they are coupled with the power of the Holy Spirit and the love of a healthy community. Here's your first one!

--Forgiveness Pearl--

> "Father, thank you for forgiving me. It's because you first forgave me that now I can also forgive (Name of the Person)."
>
> "(Name of the Person), I forgive you for the lies that the enemy brought to my heart because of your actions or words." [Listen to the Holy Spirit, as He will show you the lies that came to you. Allow yourself to be led by Him. These lies can be about yourself, your dreams, your views of God, your relationships, your Calling and Destiny, etc.]
>
> "(Name of the Person), I forgive you for introducing fear into my life, specifically the fears of ____." [Examples of specific fears are: fear of failure, fear of not being good enough, fear of men, fear of vulnerability and connection with others, etc. As you go through this, you fill in the blanks]
>
> "(Name of the Person), I forgive you for leaving me vulnerable and opening the door to _____." [Examples: depression, shame, self-hatred, anger, the occult, sexual immorality, rejection, etc. Be led by the Holy Spirit as you go through this. Choose to trust Him. Allow him to lead you.}]
>
> "(Name of the Person), I forgive you for the shortage or total absence of _____."
> [Examples: protection, affection, stability, love, kindness, etc. Make sure to list out all that apply to you and have negatively affected your soul.]

> "(Name of the Person), I forgive you for the heartache and pain that I have carried or struggled with until now." [Sometimes, that means all of your life. Make sure that you are letting this go. Be purposeful and intentional even if you're not "feeling the feelings"! Allow your Spirit to lead you and believe that your emotions/feelings will follow.]
>
> "(Name of the Person), I forgive you, I release you, and I bless you."
>
> Bless and pray for the individual that you have forgiven. Make up blessings over their life and declare them aloud until you've run out of blessings. [You can't go wrong with this!]
>
> *Stop, be very still, and take a few deep breaths.*

{Note to the Leader: Encourage the women around the one who is forgiving to stay sensitive to the basic needs around her like tissues, water, taking three seconds to breathe, or even just a pause for a long hug. This may be harder for some, so encourage your group to be tender to Holy Spirit's prompting, although <u>this is not a time to prophesy</u>! Each woman will be receiving enough already by using this pearl.}

This exercise will take you to end of your first gathering. Don't worry if you aren't able to finish with every woman; we make time in the Second Meeting for you if you do not finish.

Dismiss all with prayer and love, hugs and kisses.

"This message is from the Lord, who stretched out the heavens, laid the foundations of the earth, and formed the human spirit."
--Zechariah 12:1 NLT--

Notes

Notes

Notes

Freedom Pearls: Meeting Two

Menu Suggestion

- Wild rice with quinoa, cranberries, and walnuts
- Ground Lamb and Chicken
- Roasted Veggie Platters (yellow and orange peppers, red onions, carrots and Brussel sprouts)
- Grapes and Strawberries (help yourself to as much as you'd like!)

What You'll Need

- <u>Blessing Your Spirit</u> by Gunter & Burk
- Bluetooth Speaker

Schedule

- Welcome & Spirit Blessing [20 minutes]
- Forgiveness Pearl Wrap-Up (if needed)
- A Godly Way to Grieve Pearl, Part 1 [30 minutes]
- Dinner, Dessert, & Table Talks [1 hour, 30 minutes]
- Bathroom Break [10 minutes]
- A Godly Way to Grieve Pearl, Part 2 [Remaining Time]

Welcome & Spirit Blessing [20 min]

This is meeting number two and now the expectancy that "this is going to get deep" is prominent in the room. So, encourage the women to sit comfortably as you welcome everyone in and start the soaking music to read a Spirit Blessing over them. Grab your "Blessing your Spirit" book and read Day Six. Take your time through this.

Forgiveness Pearl Wrap-up (if needed)

After finishing the Spirit Blessing, gently transition to completing any forgiveness exercise that was left unfinished from Meeting One. (See the Forgiveness Pearl box copied again below.) Stand in agreement with each woman at the end of their forgiveness time. Don't rush through this. Take as much time as needed.

--Forgiveness Pearl--

"Father, thank you for forgiving me. It's because you first forgave me that now I can also forgive (Name of the Person)."

"(Name of the Person), I forgive you for the lies that the enemy brought to my heart because of your actions or words." [Listen to the Holy Spirit, as He will show you the lies that came to you. Allow yourself to be led by Him. These lies can be about yourself, your dreams, your views of God, your relationships, your Calling and Destiny, etc.]

"(Name of the Person), I forgive you for introducing fear into my life, specifically the fears of _____." [Examples of specific fears are: fear of failure, fear of not being good enough, fear of men, fear of vulnerability and connection with others, etc. As you go through this, you fill in the blanks]

"(Name of the Person), I forgive you for leaving me vulnerable and opening the door to _____." [Examples: depression, shame, self-hatred, anger, the occult, sexual immorality, rejection, etc. Be led by the Holy Spirit as you go through this. Choose to trust Him. Allow him to lead you.}]

"(Name of the Person), I forgive you for the shortage or total absence of _____." [Examples: protection, affection, stability, love, kindness, etc. Make sure to list out all that apply to you and have negatively affected your soul.]

"(Name of the Person), I forgive you for the heartache and pain that I have carried or struggled with until now." [Sometimes, that means all of your life. Make sure that you are letting this go. Be purposeful and intentional even if you're not "feeling the feelings"! Allow your Spirit to lead you and believe that your emotions/feelings will follow.]

"(Name of the Person), I forgive you, I release you, and I bless you."

> Bless and pray for the individual that you have forgiven. Make up blessings over their life and declare them aloud until you've run out of blessings. [You can't go wrong with this!]
>
> *Stop, be very still, and take a few deep breaths.*

{Note to the Leader: Encourage the women around the one who is forgiving to stay sensitive to the basic needs around her like tissues, water, taking three seconds to breathe, or even just a pause for a long hug. This may be harder for some, so encourage your group to be tender to Holy Spirit's prompting, although <u>this is not a time to prophesy</u>! Each woman will be receiving enough already by using this pearl.}

A Godly Way to Grieve Pearl, Part 1 [30 min]

Now it's time for your second Freedom Pearl: A Godly Way to Grieve!

Although grieving is a part of human life, it should never take all of your life. So, we believe that Godly grieving has a beginning, a middle, and an end. We also know that this process is different for everyone and, although difficult, really important.

> *"Blessed are those who mourn, for they shall be comforted."*
> **--Matthew 5:4 (ESV)--**

--A Godly Way to Grieve Pearl, Part 1--

> Play *"Have Courage" by Justin Byrne* (Song #10 on his album *Dreaming in Color*) on repeat.
>
> Lead the women in the following exercise.
>
> *Say: "Choose one subject and completely recognize your pain and suffering. Allow it to come to you. Don't make it a small deal. Try your best to embrace it, instead of making it "disappear. You might already start feeling it hurt; fully acknowledge it. Pray this: 'Father God, I give you full permission to show me and instruct me in your way of grieving. Take me through this process with you. I believe your promise that as I mourn, I will be comforted and blessed.'"*

> Pause for a few minutes and let the women pray.
>
> *Say: "Openly, pour out your sufferings to the Lord. Psalm 62:8 [NIV] says 'Trust in [God] at all times, you people; pour out your hearts to him, for God is our refuge.' Take a few minutes to allow your heart to connect to God with your pain. Take some deep breaths and grab your journal."*
>
> Pause for a few minutes to allow the ladies to follow your instructions.
>
> *Say: "Now, as you listen to the soaking music, write a letter to God in your journal describing how you feel and what you're feeling. Be as honest as you can with your pain."*
>
> Give **20 minutes** for the women to do this.

This pearl has been divided into two parts, with dinner in the middle. (We did this because it is long and we cannot emphasize enough the importance of taking your time with this. So, don't rush Part One, eat and share, and then take your time on Part Two.)

Dinner & Dessert [1 hour, 30 min]

Once everyone is served, guide the women into a dinner table exercise:

Table Talks [During Dinner]

During dinner, make time for everyone to "share their pain". Each woman will share the pain they processed with the Lord, what they wrote that needed grieving, and how the Lord is moving. Have the group pray in agreement and seal what God did in their Spirit as they pray and prophesy over each woman in turn.

Quick Bathroom Break [10 min]

As a host, take this time to take the food back to the kitchen and clear the dining table from dishes. Run a fresh pot of coffee or tea and refresh or refill the water dispenser.

A Godly Way to Grieve Pearl, Part 2 [The remaining time you have]

After the break, transition back to the dining room, put the soaking music back on, and encourage the women to sit comfortably and close to their small group, so that they can continue working on this together. Lead them by in the second part of the Godly Way to Grieve Pearl:

--A Godly Way to Grieve Pearl, Part 2--

Say: "Revelation 21:4 [NKJV] says 'And God will wipe away every tear from their eyes; there shall be no more death, nor sorrow, nor crying. There shall be no more pain, for the former things have passed away.' As you meditate on this passage, know that God cares a great deal about your every tear and your every sorrow."

Give them about **5 minutes** (or more, depending on how much time you have) to meditate on this verse.

*Say: "Now, recognize ways that you have tried to deal with this grief on your own and write them down in your journal. They can be good things (like talking to pastors, therapy, opening up to friends, etc.) or negative things too (like turning to addictions, avoidance, workaholism, busyness, anything to numb the pain, etc.). Be open about this. No one else will read this and you will not be judged. This is truly about opening up your heart before the Father."

Say: "Continue talking to God about your suffering. And look for His help until you have received His coordinates on how to navigate this. Don't rush this process."

Give them about **10 minutes** (or more, depending on how much time you have) to write these things down.

*Say: "In your journal, now write a letter from *God* to *you*! Let him speak to you and show you how He wants to walk you through this process. When He speaks, *obey*. This only works when you are willing to follow Him, no matter how He guides you. Trust Him. This is going to get really good!" [Note to the Leader: For this pearl, you will need extra tissues {and extra hugs}. It's tough to acknowledge pain.]*

Give them about **10 minutes** (or more, depending on how much time you have) to process this.

> Say: "Persevere. Don't stop this healing process, until the Lord delivers you. You will feel lighter and Hope will arise. Make sure to repeat this process with other issues that require grieving. You will feel freedom each step of the way."

When you've reached your 5 hour limit, it is time to end the meeting. Each woman will be processing this in a different way. Some will stay quiet and be ready to go home. Others will want to stay longer and process a bit more with Jesus, soaking in His goodness. Others may want to talk to you about what they just went through or they may need to stay in their small group. Others might just need a hug. {Healing hugs are at least 12 seconds long}

"And I will give you a new heart, and I will put a new spirit in you. I will take out your stony, stubborn heart and give you a tender, responsive heart."
--Ezekiel 36:26 NLT--

Notes

Notes

Notes

Freedom Pearls: Meeting Three

Menu Suggestion

- Croque Monsieur {It's super easy! Don't be intimidated by a French name.}
- Squash and Corn Creamy Soup {Which means EVERYTHING is blended!}
- Spinach Salad with shaved Brussel Sprouts, Mango, and Almonds
- Dessert: Walnut Brownies and a Bowl of Fresh Cherries {or any seasonal fruit}
- Drink: Pineapple Juice and Ginger Ale Punch with Pieces of Pineapple and Mint

What You'll Need

- <u>Blessing Your Spirit</u> by Burke & Gunther
- Your Bible
- <u>Hinds' Feet on High Places</u> (Children's version) by Hannah Hunnard
- Different Disposable Goods (to set up your dining table differently from the previous weeks)
- Mini Flower Arrangements spread around the tables, serving area, and meeting room {And don't forget one in the bathroom!}
- Bluetooth Speaker

Schedule

- Welcome & Spirit Blessing [15 minutes]
- Exercise One: Overcoming a Victim Mentality/Spirit [45 minutes]
- Getting Rid of Lies Pearl [50 minutes]
- Hinds' Feet on High Places Reading [40 minutes]
- Dinner & Table Talks [1 hour, 30 minutes]
- Bathroom Break [10 minutes]
- Hinds' Feet on High Places Reading #2 [40 minutes]
- Ending [5 minutes]

Welcome & Spirit Blessing [15 min]

This meeting will begin in the meeting room. As everyone arrives, greet everyone with a hug {any hug worth giving should take more than 10 seconds because then it releases healing endorphins} and a kiss and making eye contact.

As soon as everyone is seated, start to play *I'm Not Alone by Justin Byrne.* (Song #7 from his album, *Dreaming in Color.* Remember to leave the song on repeat mode.) While the music is playing in the background at a low volume, invite the women to sit back, get comfortable, and close their eyes as you read "Spirit Blessing Day 11" over them from Blessing Your Spirit.

When you finish reading, ask the women to respond with their spirit. They will put their hands on their heart and repeat after you: "I receive these blessings and I seal them in my spirit in Jesus' name." As they continue in this same mode, read over everyone Psalm 27:5-6 and have seal it in their spirit in the same way.

Exercise One: Overcoming a Victim Mentality/Spirit [45 min]

Open the exercise with: "Can God possibly bless us with problems?"

Read 1 Peter 1:5-6.

Lead the women to asking Holy Spirit the following question below. Have them write down in their journals both the question and the answers.

"God, what are the areas in my life where you want to show yourself strong and help me overcome troubles/hardship?"

Allow the women to search the heart of Holy Spirit as they soak to the song and then begin writing down their response. Turn the volume much louder and let the song play through twice. This should take no more than **15 minutes**.

Turn the volume down and ask the second question. Have the women write down the question and answers just like before.

"God, how do you want me to seek you regarding these problems?"

Turn the music louder and have them write down their answers as you play through it twice. Again, this should take no more than **15 minutes**.

Change the song to *A Strong Wind* (Song #3 on the same album) and turn the volume down. Ask the third question and have them write, the same as before.

"Holy Spirit, would you show me all of the lies that I have believed about my hardship along with the troubles, anxieties, and fears that have kept me bound, in harm or maybe even sick (physically or emotionally)?"

Turn the music louder and allow the women a good **10 minutes** to write down those answers. Get rid of the lies. Replace them with truth!

Getting Rid of Lies Pearl [50 min]

Here is your next Freedom Pearl!

--Getting Rid of Lies Pearl—

> After we've identified what has been coming against us to steal our joy, we need to take these thoughts captive through Jesus. Lead the women through the following Pearl, having them repeat after you. "In the name of Jesus, I nail to the cross _____." [Fill in the blanks with thoughts, feelings, or emotions that Holy Spirit brought up when you asked these questions.]
>
> "I break all agreements that I have made with these lies (List them out again), in any way known or unknown to me. And I ask you, Jesus, to forgive me for agreeing with those lies."
>
> "Father God, I ask you to take these lies far away from me, in the name of Jesus."
>
> *"Holy Spirit, what do you want to give me to replace these lies?"* [Take a few quiet moments to receive from God. Be sure to write your truths down.] *"God, how do you want to use me under the influence of your truth and your spirit to bless and release faith and encouragement to others?"*
>
> Say (but with no repetition): "The moment you receive truth, it immediately replaces a lie. Even if you're not feeling any different, the spirit realm is real and truth defines your identity. And from that moment on, you are empowered to give to others. You are equipped to overflow!!"}

> Instruct (no repetition): "Be specific with God about this! Get practical downloads that make you a powerful person."

Turn the music off. After all that writing, have the women stand up, yawn, and stretch a bit!

Hinds' Feet on High Places Reading #1 [40 min]

Have the women sit back down again. Read Chapter 1 and half of Chapter 2 of Hinds' Feet on High Places. Use the children's version of the book and show them the pictures as you go. The reason I recommend the children's version because it is simple and beautifully illustrated, yet it still conveys such greatness and wisdom.

Dinner [1 hour, 30 min]

Gather everyone into the dining room and bless the meal.

Table Talks [during dinner]

At dinner, have the women share what they wrote in their small groups.

After each woman shares, the whole group gets to stand in agreement with the truths they've received, sealing it in their spirit as you pray and prophesy. Dinner today takes about 90 minutes. Give this time for it is very significant and a lot of women will be receiving new identity.

Bathroom Break [10 minutes]

After dinner, have a bathroom break for the ladies and regroup in the meeting room. Take dessert and maybe coffees and teas. {Make sure that this transition takes no more than 10 minutes.}

Hinds' Feet on High Places Reading #2 [40 min]

Back in the room, cozy and eating sugar, continue reading <u>Hinds' Feet on High Places</u>. Have the women settle down and enter a restful place, quietly listening as you read the rest of Chapter Two and all of Chapter Three. Don't worry, the women will be blessed and paying close attention.

Ending [5 minutes]

Wrap the meeting up by reading 1 Peter 1:2 in The Passion Translation. Have the women stand up and open their hands to receive as you read it aloud over them:

"You are not forgotten, for you have been chosen and destined by Father God. The Holy Spirit has set you apart to be God's holy ones, obedient followers of Jesus Christ who have been gloriously sprinkled with his blood. May God's delightful grace and peace cascade over you many times over!"
-- 1 Peter 1:2 TPT—

The meeting has ended. Give hugs and kisses and dismiss everybody.

"For the word of God is alive and powerful. It is sharper than the sharpest two-edged sword, cutting between soul and spirit, between joint and marrow. It exposes our innermost thoughts and desires. Nothing in all creation is hidden from God. Everything is naked and exposed before his eyes."
--Hebrews 4:12-13a NLT--

Notes

Notes

Notes

Freedom Pearls: Meeting Four

Menu Suggestion

- Salmon with Lemon & Broccolini and Asiago Cheese Tortellini
- Salad: Green bib lettuce, Asian salad mix, sesame dressing with lime and lemon pepper
- Dessert: Avocado Cream with Lime Zest
- Drink: Grape juice, Raspberry Sparkling Water, Cinnamon Sticks and Orange Slices {all together!}

What You'll Need

- Blessing Your Spirit by Arthur Burke & Sylvia Gunther
- Hinds' Feet on High Places (Children's version) by Hannah Hunnard
- Different disposable goods to set up a different dining table
- If possible, shop for different scented candles for the next two weeks!
- Bluetooth Speaker

Schedule

- Welcome & Hinds' Feet on High Places Reading [1 hour, 30 minutes]
- Prophetic Teaching [1 hour]
- Dinner & Table Talk [1 hour, 15 minutes]
- Bathroom Break [10 minutes]
- Dessert & Exercise: Dreaming With God [45 minutes]
- Closing [15 minutes]

Welcome & Hinds' Feet on High Places Reading [1 hour, 30 min]

Greet everyone and have them sit comfortably around the living room. Pray and bless your time together, then put on any song from Justin Byrne's album *Dreaming in Color* and keep the whole album on repeat. You will read for the next **hour and a half** out of Hinds' Feet on High Places.

Please make sure that you have a glass of water near you. Read with an intonation that keeps people interested and connected. For some of you, this might be harder than others. A good way to prepare is to practice the pages that you will be reading as if you are reading to children or giving a speech.

After the hour and a half of reading, have everyone stand up and stretch. Announce that you are now going to give a teaching on the prophetic.

Prophetic Teaching [1 hour]

Have the women sit down again and get comfortable and begin to teach the following. (Note: This study was given to us by my sister Raquel Borin; this is my arrangement from that study she gave to us.)

"Now, dear brothers and sisters, regarding your question about the special abilities the Spirit gives us. I don't want you to misunderstand this. You know that when you were still pagans, you were led astray and swept along in worshiping speechless idols."
--1 Corinthians 12:1-2 NLT--

Familiarity oftentimes breeds religion. It just doesn't ring as good news anymore. Prophecy can change that. Scripture is very clear about certain things regarding prophecy, such as:

First and foremost, **our God speaks.** The reason He speaks is because He is a person. He speaks from his mind, from his heart, his Holy Spirit, and his Holy Character. We practice our spiritual gifts in love through his Holy Spirit.

"So you should earnestly desire the most helpful gifts. But now let me show you a way of life that is best of all."
--1 Corinthians 12:31 NLT—

1. This Scripture is the lead-in to 1 Corinthians 13: the chapter on LOVE! Without love I AM nothing! Without the gift, I have nothing, but without **love** I am nothing. If you don't have love, prophecy becomes your identity, not your gift.
2. The purpose of prophecy is to love people. It's to reflect God!
3. As He lifts you up, you see better—you change on how you see God.

Secondly, Scripture is very clear that **we are supposed to have a desire to hear God.** Make yourself a good checklist of the motives of your heart's condition based on 1 Corinthians 13. Check if it is patient, kind, not envious, hurtful, perseverant…

"Let two or three people prophesy, and let the others evaluate what is said."
--1 Corinthians 14:29 NLT--

We see that Scripture is very clear about prophecy. We are called to prophesy, but many people don't know how. Here are a few Biblical guidelines for how to prophesy:

1. **Follow the way of love.**
2. Prophecy is taking a vertical conversation into a horizontal connection. "Father, what are you saying about this person?"
3. **Prophecy is for strengthening, encouragement, and comfort, to edify and build up both the church and the world! (1 Corinthians 14)**
4. God cares more about you building a history with Him than He does about you flowing in spiritual gifts, but He does want to give you spiritual gifts as you build history with Him.
5. **The prophetic calls out what is not as if it was!** When someone gives you a word that is really right on, tell them! Give feedback and ask for feedback when you prophesy.
6. Say it with your mouth and believe it with your heart. It will happen.
7. God is triune, so are we: body, soul, and spirit.
8. We don't renew our minds to have good thoughts; we renew our minds to know God's will.

"Dear brothers and sisters, if I should come to you speaking in an unknown language, how would that help you? But if I bring you a revelation or some special knowledge or prophecy or teaching, that will be helpful. Even lifeless instruments like the flute or the harp must play the notes clearly, or no one will recognize the melody. And if the bugler doesn't sound a clear call, how will the soldiers know they are being called to battle? It's the same for you. If you speak to people in words they don't understand, how will they know what you are saying? You might as well be talking into empty space. There are many different languages in the world, and every language has meaning. But if I don't understand a language, I will be a foreigner to someone who speaks it,

and the one who speaks it will be a foreigner to me."
--1 Corinthians 14:6-11 NLT--

As we can see from this verse, the reason we prophesy is to make God no longer a foreigner to people. **Prophecy is translating God.**

What is the connection between prophecy and faith? Well, every time you are going to prophesy, you need faith. The testimony of Jesus is prophecy. Get in the word. Get around prophetic people. Receive impartation and believe it!

"My sheep listen to my voice; I know them, and they follow me. I give them eternal life, and they will never perish. No one can snatch them away from me."
--John 10:27,28 NLT--

"If the first covenant had been faultless, there would have been no need for a second covenant to replace it...When God speaks of a "new" covenant, it means he has made the first one obsolete. It is now out of date and will soon disappear.
--Hebrews 8:7,13 NLT--

Now that we have learned the basics of how to prophesy, let us dive in to the different ways to hear God's voice. Each person hears him a bit differently, and there are strengths and weaknesses to both. It is important for us to learn what "prophetic personality" (or personalities) we carry.

4 Ways to Hear God's Voice

1. Knower
    I. These people just "know". People will ask: "Did God tell you?" And they reply: "No. I just know." In Acts 16, Paul chose Timothy because he "knew".
    II. Knowers' Attributes:
        a. Knowers have intuitive sense impressions
        b. Knowers are commonly right about the outcome
        c. Knowers believe that the Word is like the end all
    III. Knowers' Strengths:
        a. Knowers will push through some things, some obvious barriers for what you know.
        b. Knowers have tenacity to push through!
        c. Knowers' know that relationships are not always more important than the end result.
    IV. Knowers' Weaknesses:
        a. Knowers can have a hard time valuing others who hear God differently

b. Knowers can leave others behind.
2. Seer
   I. 1 Chronicles 29:29 NLT says: "All the events of David's reign, from beginning to end, are written in *The Record of Samuel the Seer, The Record of Nathan the Prophet,* and *The Record of Gad the Seer.*"
   II. Seers' Attributes:
      a. Seers are visionaries / dreamers (day or night)
      b. Seers have the ability to see
      c. Seers think "If you can't picture it, you aren't passionate".
   III. Seers' Strengths:
      a. Seers see past what most people can't see to show you your future
      b. Seers think big
      c. Seers speak forth the impossible
   IV. Seers' Weaknesses:
      a. Seers can have a hard time handling the small things
      b. Seers can have a hard time with those who don't see
      c. Sometimes seers have to wait.
3. Hearer
   I. Hearers' Attributes
      a. Hearers always know
      b. Hearers work independently and focused
      c. Hearers keep the Word in front of them
      d. Hearers have a special way of hearing God, remembrance
      e. Hearers often have lots of journals
      f. Hearers point to specific periods of time when God spoke to them.
   II. Hearers' Strengths:
      a. Hearers are focused; they ask for the one thing
      b. Hearers work independently to keep the words they have heard
   III. Hearers' Weaknesses:
      a. Hearers can cloud the message with the messenger
      b. Hearers lose the huge word in the details
4. Feeler
   I. Feelers' Attributes
      a. Feelers have key insight to the heart of God!
      b. Feelers can't always explain what God is doing, but feels it.
   II. Feelers' Strengths
      a. Feelers can "CATCH" spiritual moments most people miss
      b. Once feelers encounter a *word*, they stop.

c. Feelers can walk into the room and feel what God is doing (radars)
    III.   Feelers' Weaknesses
                a. Feelers can get too caught up in emotions
                b. Feelers can be labeled as emotional
                c. Feelers can overvalue their feelings

We can all be more than 1 or 2, but we all carry at least 1 prophetic personality. God speaks to each differently, but the truth is **we need each other**.

Pause, turn the volume up on your soaking music, and ask your Freedom Pearls this question:

"Father what are my blessings in times of transition? What do you give me for this time and what do you want to say to me about this time?"

Pause and then read this over the women: "Daniel 2:21 says 'He changes times and seasons, He disposes kings and raises up others. He gives wisdom to the wise and knowledge to the discerning.'"

Give the women time to journal the answers to the questions and then release them to dinner.

Dinner & Table Talks [1 hour and 15 minutes]

Pray for the meal and serve. After everyone is seated and eating, instruct the women to share with their small group the answers from their soaking while they eat.

Bathroom Break [10 minutes]

After dinner, have a bathroom break for the ladies and regroup in the meeting room. Take dessert and maybe coffees and teas. {Make sure that this transition takes no more than 10 minutes.}

Dessert & Exercise One: Dreaming With God [45 min]

After dinner, grab a dessert and come sit back down in your comfy meeting space. Put on any of the soaking songs and read <u>Blessing Your Spirit</u> #19 "Friends During Transition" - A change from God's old order to God's new order.

Read the spirit blessing over the women as the soaking songs play.

Next, give the women these instructions: "Anything you can accomplish with hard work, diligence and self-effort is not the kind of God dream that we are looking for. We are looking for dreams that are so impossible that, unless God breathes on it, it can't happen. {Literally: A MIRACLE!} If money was not an impediment and you could dream without a ceiling about *anything* what would it be? Write this in your journal and ask, *"Holy Spirit, would you awaken dreaming with God in my heart?"*

Next, play the song *Orchestrated* from the album *Dreaming in Color* by Justin Byrne three times. The first time, ask the women to just imagine and dream with God. They can lean back, lie on a couch or pillow, or on the floor. It's all about getting comfortable and soaking with the Holy Spirit into your dreaming.

The second time the song plays, instruct the women to start journaling ALL that comes to them.

The third time the song plays, encourage them to go even deeper into dreaming the dreams of God with God.

The exercise after the Spirit Blessing should only take about **15 minutes**.

Closing [15 min]

Close the night with a prayer that releases an impartation for dreaming in the night, as God continues what He started in the soaking time. Encourage the women to record in their journals any dream they get in the night. {If they're too groggy or half asleep, suggest that they record a voice memo into their phones. It helps to journal later!} Give hugs and kisses and encourage the women to go home and continue dreaming in the night.

SPECIAL NOTE: Before you dismiss the women, prep them for Meeting Five by saying, "Please do not wear any makeup for our next meeting. But do bring your makeup bag." And remind them of that by text one night before Meeting Five. {Some women will not like this; encourage them anyhow. Tell them that it will be a great surprise.}

Then, wish them Good Night!

> "throw off your old sinful nature and your former way of life, which is corrupted by lust and deception. Instead, let the Spirit renew your thoughts and attitudes. Put on your new nature, created to be like God—truly righteous and holy."
> **--Ephesians 4:22-24 NLT--**

Notes

Notes

Notes

Freedom Pearls: Meeting Five – "No Masks"

Menu Suggestion

- For this final meeting, use your creativity and plan a meal. This can be something that you are "famous" for in your household or something completely new to you. Remember to have desserts and drinks and to change the table settings a bit, such as a new table cloth or different disposable goods, candles, flowers, etc.

What You'll Need

- <u>Blessing Your Spirit</u> by Arthur Burke & Sylvia Gunther
- <u>Hinds' Feet on High Places</u> (Children's version) by Hannah Hunnard
- A concert {yes… I know that it's a stretch, but you heard me right… a concert.}
    - You will certainly have to plan ahead, maybe even reach out to friends from your church community who play instruments. Be creative and, more importantly, be led by the Holy Spirit on who to pick and what exactly will happen. This concert should take about one hour. You can plan for worshippers to come to your home or, if it is nearby, you can take your group of Freedom Pearls over to the musician's house—it all depends on what you arrange and what is doable logistically. This is all about blessing their Spirit through worship, song, sound, and music.
- Arrange for a photographer to be there for 20 minutes.
    - The photographer will not need to be long. That should probably be toward the final 2 hours of the meeting, not the first 3.
- Prepare a tray of a variety of blank notes for the women to choose from. {These can be easily found at Target or craft stores}
- Small containers and lids {you can buy these at Party City}, each filled with two very full tablespoons of facial masks {I bought ours at Target and chose two different types}
- A pack of jumbo popsicle sticks {I bought these at Hobby Lobby, but any craft store near you will do.}
- A packet of facial wipes {Also at Target}
- A face-sized hand-mirror & enough mirror space for all the women to look at the same time
    - NOTE: You might need extra mirrors if your home does not have enough mirror space for all of the women in your group.
- A whole tray of warm and wet, new washcloths with two drops of lavender oil {These will go in the oven to keep warm; remember to prep them ahead of time!}
- Bluetooth Speaker

Schedule

- Welcome & Hinds' Feet on High Places Reading [50 minutes]
- Spirit Blessing & "No Mask" Exercise [2 hours, 30 minutes]
- Dinner Time [50 minutes]
- Photo Shoot [20 minutes]
- The Concert [25 minutes]
- Final Blessing [5 minutes]

Welcome & Hinds' Feet on High Places Reading [50 min]

As the women arrive, greet them and put on the song *Memories* by Justin Byrne from his album *The Rest of Life*. Leave it on repeat at a very low volume.

Grab the book, Hinds feet on High Places and continue reading. It should take you about **50 minutes** of reading to finish the book from where you previously left off. Once you have finished reading, keep the women gathered in your meeting room, listening to the soaking music and relaxing. Please be sure to instruct them to keep silent ("No talking") for about two minutes.

Use this brief moment to turn on your oven to 400 F and warm up your washcloths. (Set a 15-minute timer!)

Spirit Blessing & "No Mask" Exercise [2 hours, 30 min]

While the washcloths start getting warmed up, read Spirit Blessing #27: Friends in Times of Pruning from Blessing Your Spirit. After you've read and sealed this in their Spirit, grab the beautiful tray that you've prepared with the facial masks and things that you will need.

Also, turn off the oven, but leave the washcloths inside.

Say this over the women: "I have the courage to continue living with no masks, walking in vulnerability and saying no to shame." Now, you will instruct them to make their way to the center, where you will have a little table with all of the supplies that they will need. Every woman needs a partner for this exercise. You will want to have consulted Holy Spirit and set these pairs up prior to their arrival.

Each woman should take one mask, two facial wipes, and one jumbo popsicle stick. They will need to find a place within your home where one can lie down and the other can apply the mask. {Tip: Make it easier for them by setting up "stations" for them: throw pillows on the floor, towels on the bed, a towel on the side of the couch, etc. This will help them know where to go and make sure that half of the group has a place to lay down. For example, if you have 8 women, you will have 4 spots for them to lie down.}

Now that each pair is at their station, instruct the women in an audible voice:

1. "One of you will lie down while the other one will serve the one that is laying. Take the facial wipes and wipe that face down as you pray and bless her Spirit."
2. "Second, will come the mask. Take the popsicle stick and apply the mask. Apply it to the whole face, leaving the eye area clear. While applying the mask, be sure to continue praying and prophesying over that woman in an audible voice. This is ministry time and she MUST hear you."
3. "Once the application of the mask is all done, slowly get up and swap places."
4. "Repeat the process for the next pearl laying down."
5. "Once both facial masks are on, take a fun picture together."
    a. {When you see them wrapping up the facial mask process, as a good host, make sure to collect all of the garbage around them and bring the hot washcloths out to a central table/area.}
6. "Each of you grab your own warm washcloth and find a mirror. Now, as you remove your mask, look full into the mirror, blessing your Spirit and enjoying what you see.
    a. {Remember, in case you do not have enough mirror space in your home for all of the women in your group, plan ahead.}

This whole facial moment should take about **30 minutes** (approximately 15 minutes for each woman). As a leader, make sure to stay on top of that.

Each woman should now take **5-10 minutes** to apply her own makeup. {They might really want to because we will be taking pictures later. Take the same song off repeat and continue playing *The Rest of Life*.}

Gather the women in a circle and have a face-sized hand-mirror. {This exercise is deep, so make sure that you've got tissues ready!}

Passing the mirror around the circle, ask each woman to hold the mirror and look deeply into their own eyes for just a few seconds. Now, instruct them with: "Tell us what you see."

In order for this exercise to be successful, I'd like to ask the leader (yes, that's you!) to go first. Then, pass the mirror to your right.

As the leader, be prepared: some women will get very emotional and go deep with the exercise. You might see lots of crying or even hyperventilating. Give them time to breathe, tissues, and maybe a glass of cold water. But *don't* allow this to become personal ministry time by other women who feel moved—the only people who should be speaking are you and the woman with the mirror. This exercise in itself is very healing. So, bless the woman's Spirit and encourage them to keep going when it gets hard. Tell them, "Jesus will shine through your own eyes. You've got to pass through pain in order to get to your breakthrough on the other side. Persevere!"

It should be **three and a half hours** into our meeting at this point once all the women are finished.

Dinner Time [50 minutes]

After the mirror gets back into your hands, ask the women to grab their journals, pens, and a notecard from your tray and bring them to the dinner table.

As you eat dinner, ask the women to think and write a note or word of encouragement for the woman who was their partner in the "No Mask" Exercise. Tell them to "write down what Holy Spirit shows you about the other woman on that card." After everyone is done writing their note, instruct them to open their journals and write this down: "I commit to living my life more vulnerably. Letting go of my old masks. Knowing I am accepted and loved by my Father, just as I am. I say yes to taking risks, as I believe I will find a safe place to be me and not shamed or judged, as I want to do the same for others. I want to be a safe place for others too." (Dinner should take about **50 minutes** but no longer than that.)

NOTE: Dessert will be served with your music concert so, plan an easy dessert. I have found that one dessert for each woman individually is ideal.

Photography Shoot [20 min]

As dinner ends, your photographer should have arrived and prepped for a set of group photos. Once the ladies are done eating, take them to where you will have the photos. This should not take more than **20 minutes**.

The Concert [25 min]

Reorganize your ladies and get that concert going! {If you are driving, try to fit everyone in one car or assign people into specific car rides. The fewer cars, the better.}

If your concert is coming to your home, make sure to make room and accommodations for that. (They can be setting up while photos are being taken)

This should be music that blesses the soul. Think old traditional hymns, classics, or something deep where the women can soak it all in and enjoy dessert. The dessert for that meeting should be something easy to eat—think cupcakes, cookies, or anything that you can savor with a napkin while listening to the concert.

As the leader, you can use the concert time as an opportunity to go around the room praying over the women, as Holy Spirit leads you. If you are going somewhere else for the concert, remember to bring dessert along with you or make plans for the person hosting the concert to help with dessert. The coffee, tea, and water station should also be available.

After the concert, we have almost reached the end of session five.

Father's Blessing [5 min]

The following blessing is a direct transcript from my father, Gui Kerr's, original message to us at our first Freedom Pearls. It is a powerful way to end your time with your Freedom Pearls.

Say "If you've never received a blessing from your earthly father, stand up. If you have, stay seated. If you have not, stand up and prepare to receive."

Read the following out loud to your Freedom Pearls:

"I call your spirit to full attention to connect with the Holy Spirit and take heed of the Word of God for you. I bless your spirit with the blessing of a father, standing as a father on behalf of your own father, if you would allow me. I bless you with the blessings that were yours from Father God but may or may not have arrived safely at your door.

I bless you with protection that only the presence of the Father in the house can bring: the full assurance that you are cared for and precious in your Father's eyes, that He would lay down His life for your sake, as indeed He did, that He would leave ninety-nine in safety and steadily pursue the one that went astray, that even when your earthly father and mother forsake you, He would never leave you or forsake you. I bless you with grasping the depth of His protection over you like someone who finds shelter in a strong tower and hides under the shadow of the highest of all. I bless you with the peace that comes from that level of protection, the certainty that you can literally walk through the valley of the shadow of death and fear no evil, for you know that you know that your Father is with you.

I bless you with the blessing of provision that Father God brings. I bless you with understanding the economy of heaven, for generosity starts at the top and trickles down to every nook and cranny of the Kingdom of the Son of his Love. I bless you with all that you have, every provision, not only financial, but physical: your strengths, emotional: your sensibilities, spiritual: your gifts and your talents. I bless you to embrace all that as a true gift from on high, from the Father of Lights in whom there is no shadow or change. I bless you with a generous heart that invites even more blessings, a heart that responds to His love and provision—not out of fear or obedience or exchange, but simply out of the abundance that you find in His presence.

Last, but not least, I bless you with the true sense of your identity that the Father instills in every one of His children. I bless you with words a good father lavishes on his daughters: that you are unique, that you are beautiful inside and out, that you were created with a purpose and for a purpose. You are a woman and I bless you in your identity as a woman, not to compete with other men or women, but to rejoice in and enjoy your uniqueness.

I speak to your spirit: you're a beautiful daughter, there is no other daughter like you. You have it in you to be kind, to be captivating, and to be loyal. You are wise, and you are able to choose well. You are strong and more than able to make the best decisions. You are discerning and bold to sort right from wrong and choose what is right. You are aware—fully aware—of your value as you have forgiven every single person that took away from your worth, either through words, or through silence, or through actions, or all of the above. You are not defined anymore by those things and those people but by what you hear your Father say about you through His spirit every day.

I bless you to hear the Holy Spirit and walk in protection, provision, and in the fullness of your identity in the name of Jesus the Messiah. Amen."

- Papa Gui Kerr

Say: "Repeat after me: I receive this blessing and I seal it in my spirit."

Bless everyone and encourage them to get a manual, so they can reproduce Freedom Pearls Around the Table in their own home.

If you would prefer, you can purchase a manual for each of your Pearls. As you put a manual in each woman's hand, release an impartation and an anointing for creativity and reproducing this freedom in other women's lives.

God will clearly show you women that are comfortable and will easily lead FP with a manual and the ones that are feeling insecure about it. Intentionally encourage and spend a little extra time with the ones that might be insecure.

Note to the Leader: Stay connected to your pearls! Call or text them weekly for about a month. Check in to see how they are feeling, if they have received new breakthroughs, and if they are considering starting their own group. You might offer you help to start some of them off.

"So I want you to become scholars of all that is good and beautiful, and stay pure and innocent when it comes to evil. And the God of peace will swiftly pound Satan to a pulp under your feet! And the wonderful favor of our Lord Jesus will surround you.
--Romans 16:19b-20 TPT—

"Restore to me the joy of your salvation, and make me willing to obey you."
--Psalms 51:12 NLT--

Notes

Notes

Notes

Final Thoughts

As we come to an end, I'd like to help you consider that an end to one thing is definitely the beginning of something else. May the closure of these five weeks be the opening of a door to shepherd women well, taking good care of their hearts, remaining connected, CHOOSING VULNERABILITY, and being available as the Holy Spirit guides you (always ask Holy Spirit "how much time, with whom?").

I bless you to now reproduce your own values, tap in to more of your creativity—and who knows? Maybe you'll write a book, record an album, begin a YouTube channel, start a creative hub, or own a restaurant. It really doesn't matter what kind of fruits you decide to bear from this as long as you bear fruit and continue to grow, making sure to listen to Holy Spirit along the way. You cannot go wrong with this.

So, as my dad one day said to me: "If you knew that the God of the Universe has your back, how bold would you be?"

Feel free to contact me by email! Count on me as I commit to staying reachable: shaila@freedompearls.com

You can also find me on Instagram @shailakerrministries

Recipes

Meeting One
- ❖ Arugula Salad with Parmesan Cheese & Lime Vinaigrette
- ❖ Artichoke & Spinach Risotto
    - o Prep Time: 5 mins; Cook Time: 25 mins
    - o Servings: 8 servings
    - o Author: Tasty Ever After
    - o Spinach Artichoke Risotto is the ultimate in creamy and comforting goodness with all the flavors of the classic dip. This easy, cheesy, vegetarian entrée or side dish can be on the table in 30 minutes!
    - o Ingredients for the Spinach Artichoke Mixture:
        - ▪ 4 tablespoons unsalted butter
        - ▪ 1 small onion, chopped
        - ▪ 3 cups frozen chopped spinach, thawed and squeezed dry
        - ▪ 1 cup artichoke hearts, not marinated, chopped
        - ▪ 1 garlic clove, finely minced
        - ▪ ¼ teaspoon crushed red pepper, optional
        - ▪ Salt and pepper to taste
    - o Ingredients for the Risotto:
        - ▪ 7-8 cups vegetable broth or chicken broth
        - ▪ 3 tablespoons unsalted butter, divided
        - ▪ 2 cups Arborio rice
        - ▪ ¾ cup dry white wine
        - ▪ 3 cups Havarti cheese, shredded
    - o Instructions for the Spinach Artichoke Mixture:
        - ▪ Melt 4 tablespoons of butter in a heavy-bottomed large pan over medium heat. Add the onion and sauté for 2-3 minutes. Add the spinach, artichoke hearts, garlic, and crushed red pepper (optional) to the onions and sauté for another 2-3 minutes. Season with salt and pepper to taste. Remove mixture from pan and set aside.
    - o Instructions for the Risotto:
        - ▪ Heat the broth in a medium saucepan over medium-low heat and keep hot (broth must be hot before adding to rice). In the same large pan that the spinach artichoke mixture was cooked in, melt 2 tablespoons of butter over medium heat. Add the Arborio rice and cook, stirring continuously, for about 1 minute, making sure all rice is coated with the butter.

- Add the wine and stir constantly until the wine has fully absorbed into the rice, about 1-2 minutes. Add the hot broth, 1 cup at a time, to the rice and stir constantly until the broth is almost fully absorbed into the rice. Continue to add the broth until the rice is tender and the mixture is creamy, about 20-25 minutes. Add more broth for a creamier texture. Rice should be slightly al dente (firm to the bite), not mushy, and a very creamy texture.
- Reduce heat to low and stir in the Havarti cheese, the remaining 1 tablespoon of butter, and the spinach artichoke mixture. Stir well and heat through for a couple of minutes. Serve immediately.

❖ Marinated, Pan-Fried, Sliced Chicken Breast
  ○ Top each risotto dish with chicken
❖ Sparkling Water & Cranberry Punch
❖ Grapes & Strawberries
❖ Here are some photos of some of the ingredients I purchased & used:

Meeting Two

- ❖ Wild rice with quinoa, cranberries, and walnuts
- ❖ Ground Lamb and Chicken
    - o Author: Shaila Kerr
    - o Instructions:
        - Thinly dice *one whole sweet onion* & *6 cloves of garlic*
        - Sautee them in a pan with about *4 tablespoons of olive oil* until the onions are translucent and start looking caramelized
        - Add the *ground chicken* and *ground lamb*
        - Juice *1 very juicy lime* over the meat
        - Mix in:
            - *1 teaspoon of lemon pepper*
            - *3 teaspoons of salt*
            - *1 whole package of thinly chopped mint leaves*
            - *1 teaspoon of nutmeg*
            - *4 tablespoons of balsamic vinegar*
            - *1 tsp of sugar*
        - Stir this mixture on medium to high heat until all the meat looks cooked and loose
        - Tip: Do not cover it with a lid or it will produce too much liquid; constantly stir it and allow the heat to dry up the liquid
        - Always taste your food (see if you would like to add anything else)
- ❖ Roasted Veggie Platters (yellow and orange peppers, red onions, carrots, and Brussel sprouts)
    - o Photos above and to the right!
- ❖ Grapes and Strawberries (as much as you'd like!)

Meeting Three
- ❖ Croque Monsieur
  - o Ingredients for the Béchamel
    - ¼ cup (½ stick) unsalted butter
    - ¼ cup all-purpose flour
    - 1½ cups whole milk
    - 2 tablespoons whole grain mustard
    - ½ teaspoon freshly grated nutmeg or ¼ ground nutmeg
    - Kosher salt
  - o Ingredients for the Assembly
    - 8 slices ½"-thick country-style bread
    - 6 oz. ham, preferably Paris ham (about 8 slices)
    - 3 oz. Gruyère, grated (about 1½ cups)
    - 1 teaspoon Herbes de Provence
  - o Instructions for the Béchamel
    - Melt butter in a medium saucepan over medium heat until foamy.
    - Add flour and cook, stirring, until mixture is pale and foamy, about 3 minutes.
    - Gradually add milk, stirring until mixture is smooth.
    - Cook, stirring, until sauce is thick and somewhat elastic, about 4 minutes.
    - Remove from heat and whisk in mustard and nutmeg; season with salt.
    - Tip: Béchamel can be made 1 day ahead. Let cool; press plastic wrap directly onto surface and chill.
  - o Instructions for the Assembly
    - Preheat oven to 425°.
    - Spread bread slices with béchamel, dividing evenly and extending all the way to the edges.
    - Place 4 slices of bread, béchamel side up, on a parchment-lined baking sheet.
    - Top with ham and half of cheese.
    - Top with remaining slices of bread, béchamel side up, then top with remaining cheese and sprinkle with Herbes de Provence.
    - Bake until cheese is brown and bubbling, 10-15 minutes.
    - Tip: Sandwiches can be made (but not baked) 1 day ahead. Cover; chill.
- ❖ Squash and Corn Chowder (Creamy Soup)
  - o Prep Time: 20 minutes
  - o Cook Time: 20 minutes
  - o Ingredients:
    - 6 slices bacon, cooked and crumbled
    - 1 & 1/2 Tbsp rendered bacon fat reserved
    - 1 & 1/2 lbs yellow squash, chopped (about 3 medium)

- 2/3 cup thinly sliced celery
- 1 cup sliced green onions, divided
- 1 Tbsp flour
- 2 cloves garlic, minced
- 2 & 3/4 cup milk (I used 1%)
- 5 cups fresh cut corn (from about 6 ears corn), divided
- 1/2 cup heavy cream
- 1 & 1/2 tsp chopped fresh thyme (or 1/2 tsp dried)
- 3/4 tsp salt, then more to taste
- 1/4 tsp freshly ground black pepper, then more to taste if desired
- Shredded cheddar cheese, for serving

- Instructions:
    - In a large soup pot over medium-high heat, add bacon, bacon fat, onions, and celery, cooking and stirring until the onion starts to brown. Add garlic, salt, thyme and pepper and cook 1 minute.
    - Stir in broth, scraping the bottom of the pot to remove any browned bits.
    - Add potatoes and corn. Stir, bring to a simmer, and reduce heat to medium.
    - Cover and cook for 15-20 minutes until potatoes are tender. Reduce heat to low.
    - Combine milk, flour, and heavy cream and gradually whisk into soup mixture, a little at a time, until thickened slightly.
    - Serve as desired.
- Photo Below!

❖ Spinach Salad with shaved Brussel Sprouts, Mango, and Almonds
❖ Dessert: Walnut Brownies and a Bowl of Fresh Cherries {or any seasonal fruit}
❖ Drink: Pineapple Juice and Ginger Ale Punch with Pieces of Pineapple and Mint

Meeting Four

- ❖ Salmon with Lemon & Broccolini and Asiago Cheese Tortellini
  - Prep Time: 10 minutes
  - Cook Time: 35 minutes
  - Serves: 6
  - Ingredients for the Roasted Broccoli:
    - 1 1/2 pounds broccoli, cut into bite size pieces
    - 1 tablespoon olive oil
    - 1 tablespoon fresh lemon juice
    - 2 cloves garlic, chopped
    - Salt and black pepper, to taste
  - For the Tortellini:
    - 1 pound cheese tortellini, refrigerated or frozen
    - 3 tablespoons unsalted butter
    - 1 tablespoon minced shallot
    - 2 cloves garlic minced
    - Dash of crushed red pepper
    - 3 cups packed fresh spinach
    - Zest & Juice of 1 large lemon
    - 1/2 cup freshly grated Parmesan cheese
    - Salt and black pepper, to taste
  - Instructions
    - Preheat the oven to 400 degrees F. Place the broccoli pieces on a large baking sheet. Drizzle with olive oil and lemon juice. Add the garlic and toss broccoli until well coated. Season with salt and pepper, to taste. Place baking sheet in the oven and roast for 20-25 minutes, stirring once. Remove broccoli when it is crisp and slightly charred. Set aside.
    - Meanwhile, bring a large pot of salted water to a boil. Cook tortellini according to package instructions. When cooked, drain, but reserve 1/2 cup of the pasta water. Set the water and tortellini aside.
    - Put the pot back on the stove and melt the butter over medium heat. Add the shallot, garlic, crushed red pepper, and spinach and cook until spinach is wilted, about 3 minutes. Add the lemon zest and stir.
    - Turn the heat to low and add the cooked tortellini and roasted broccoli to the pot. Stir in the reserved pasta water and lemon juice. Cook on low until

tortellini is warm, about two minutes. Sprinkle Parmesan cheese over the tortellini and season with salt and pepper, to taste. Serve warm.
- ❖ Salad: Green bib lettuce, Asian salad mix, sesame dressing with lime and lemon pepper
- ❖ Dessert: Avocado Cream with Lime Zest
- ❖ Drink: Grape juice, Raspberry Sparkling Water, Cinnamon Sticks and Orange Slices {all together!}

Administrative Documents

Photo/Video Release Form

I hereby authorize _____ and those acting pursuant to his/her/its authority a nonexclusive grant to:

(a) Record my likeness and voice on video, audio, photographic, digital, electronic, online format, or on any and all other media.

(b) Use my name in connection with these recording.

(c) Use, reproduce, publish, republish, exhibit, edit, modify, or distribute, in whole or in part, these recordings in all media without compensation for any purpose that _____, and those acting pursuant to his/her/its authority, deem appropriate, including promotional or advertising efforts. These recordings may appear in a variety of formats and media now available to _____ and that may be available in the future (e.g. print publications, video tapes, CD-ROM, Internet, mobile, digital).

I hereby release _____ and those acting pursuant to his/her/its authority from liability, claims, and demands for any violation of any personal or proprietary right I may have in connection with such use, including any and all claims for libel, defamation, or invasion of privacy. I understand that all such recordings, in whatever medium, shall remain the property of - _____. I have read and fully understand the terms of this release.

Name: _____

Address: _____

City: _____

State: _____ Zip: _____

Phone: _____

Email: _____

Signature: _____ Date: _____

Parent/Guardian Signature (if under 18):

_____ Date: _____

Contact Sheet

Name	Phone	Social Media	Email

Testimonials

Before we finish, I wanted to include a few testimonials from some of the wonderful women who have finished Freedom Pearls Around the Table. Take these words of gratitude and encouragement for yourself; you WILL see the same breakthrough as God moves through you to touch other lives!

Freedom Pearls was a life-changing experience for me. The opportunity to communicate with God and journal His voice, then share within a small group at a dinner table was so precious. The most enlightening time for me was the grieving exercise. I was able to let go of some deep disappointment as I heard God's perspective on it. Listening to the other women in my group was also very special; we connected at a deep level.
--Raquel Kerr Borin, Founder of SoundWave

I feel so fortunate to have taken the first Freedom Pearls! This invitation to the table was LIFE ALTERING. I went to places within myself I had never been and deeply flossed my heart of all the trauma, fear, and insecurities I had held onto for many years. With every new layer I was able to heal and discover the gold within me. This is so beautifully done in community with other women who become your sisters; keepers of your secrets and forever linked by love and compassion. There is something SUPERNATURAL and yet very accessible about Freedom Pearls. If anyone is looking to connect with God, heal past wounds, leave victim mentality, start dreaming, sever Trauma, find identity, and start walking out the abundant life God has prepared, it is YOURS. Freedom Pearls is a key to the door that leads to wholeness.
Utterly Grateful and Forever Changed,
--Carol Gutierrez, VOUS Church Miami

The day I accepted my sister's invitation to go to Freedom Pearls, I confess that I had no idea how much I would be touched by God in that environment. I was surprised by God's infinite love and the way He was loving me through the women there.

I had noticed a difference on my sister's countenance as the weeks passed and I knew Shaila was such an amazing woman of God, but I was totally surprised as I received healing for my emotions. Jesus touched my soul as I was well-loved by all the women there: It was love without judgment, love that expects nothing in return, love that understands and is compassionate, love that feels the other's pain and that can rejoice with their joy! All I know is that since that one moment I have never been the same, for there are no arguments that can come against a real experience with God. Freedom Pearls was life-changing, by the power of God's love through those women.
--Alexandra Abrantes, Brazilian Pastor

Freedom Pearls Around the Table was a deeply beautiful experience in a small group of women that opened up my feminine heart to both receive healing in my own soul and also support others as they received their own healing. This brilliant, heaven-inspired model creates a warm, safe, and nurturing place for women to open up their hearts to God and each other. Shaila combines the elements of a lovely and inviting table, delicious and savory food, sweet fellowship with sisters in Christ, and the ministry of the Holy Spirit to heal hurting hearts. It was truly a life-changing experience for me, one I will implement myself and invite others into. I can wholeheartedly recommend Freedom Pearls Around the Table to those that desire to minister deeply to women's hearts and see them set free!
--Sharon Stark

When I saw women who are older than I opening up their hearts, it was freedom! They gave me strength to go after healing in some wounds that I didn't know were hurting me so much. To receive each of their healing hugs gave me the courage to make important decisions, which I still reap benefits from today. I have no doubt that this experience changed my life forever!
--Rebecca Coutinho

I can remember going into Freedom Pearls completely uncertain, without hope, and not even knowing that I was missing it. The time I spent in Freedom Pearls taught me to fully love who God has made me to be and to fight for the fullness of the Holy Spirit to come in power in my life. I know that, had it not come when it came, I certainly wouldn't be here, now, living out all of who God had destined and purposed for me to be. Freedom Pearls, the women there, and ABBA, through the obedience of his daughter Shaila, changed my life for the better. I am eternally grateful.
--Stephanie Jacques

Freedom Pearls does exactly what it says! Not only did it set me free from several things, but it carried over into my family and extended family. It is filled with the Holy Spirit and confirmed of promises and prayers that I didn't even know about! We are His pearls and He will go to any length to show us.
--Jamie Cheshire

It was at Freedom Pearls that my eyes were opened and I was finally able to see who I am through God's eyes. It is an experience of great exchange and vulnerability that allows us to reach the depths of our soul by reconnecting with our innermost being and with one another, restoring our true identity. Freedom Pearls was a turning point in my life!
--Carla Diaz

Freedom Pearls for me was a wonderful invitation to encounter the love and healing touch of Jesus. I felt honored and cherished in every way: delicious food, wonderful connection and

sharing transparently with sisters in Christ. Jesus met me where I was and replaced fear and grief with his love.
--Connie Sanchez

Acknowledgments

Thankful that I never had to go at it alone... & my special thanks to the following:

Rebecca Coutinho - Find a friend to help you execute it all! Someone who would love to serve with you, or could help you prep weekly, or who wants to host while you cook and teach, or who can help you with shared meals—whatever works best for you. The point here is: do it! And partner with another lady! In my case, Rebecca helped me weekly. She arrived two hours before everyone else and served with such joy and disposition. It was a great honor to have her. Her serving went from taking the trash out and chopping veggies to helping set up the table placements in special ways, making sure each woman had her name by her seat, and turning on candles before everyone arrived, praying in the room with me and setting up a spiritual atmosphere, and much more.

Stephany Jacques - I had the honor to partner with Stephany in writing this guide. Her millennial expertise and bubbly personality kept it fresh and easy, yet profound and full of truth. Her talent to write in such a time as this is undeniable and she shines in this arena.

My sister, Raquel Borin - My sister taught on one of the sessions on the prophetic for us, and it was outstanding! Helpful Tip: Find someone (a "sister") you trust and know well to speak on a session during one of the weeks. Their fresh and diverse perspective can so bless the group!

My mother, Sandra Kerr - Well, my mother taught me almost everything I know about freedom around a table. She is a master at making you feel special through a banquet at her home. She does it with grace and love and it always sets the atmosphere to reach your heart and connect deeply. My mom was not just an incredible host of our dessert time in our last session, she played piano—and for the ones in the room for that live concert that night, a little bit of Heaven opened. We will never forget! Thank you so much, Mom!!

My father, Gui Kerr - I want to thank my dad who has invested in me and called out the gold in me so many times! Thank you, dad, for speaking words of encouragement and affirmation over me. It has molded me to actually believe them! I specifically want to thank you for the blessings you so passionately declared over the women on that fifth FP meeting at the end of mom's concert time at your home. The women who were there will never forget that! It was such a beautiful, powerful, and also very prophetic moment. You are a great representation of Father God's heart to my life.

Thank you so much, both mom and dad, for believing and declaring that your rooftop would be my floor! I have believed in it, I still do, and today I also declare that for my children! It is so cool to see the power of the generational blessings of the Lord! You both are amazing and I am honored to learn so much from you two.

My husband, Igor - He was such an extreme support! He kept our boys out of the home for about seven hours each Saturday (which is a very BIG deal) and helped pay for all the expenses. His generosity is unmatched and his kindness to see people loved well is a fountain that never ceases to surprise me! Never once did he complain. He would pay compliments when the food started smelling nice and was glad to hear me share all God did as he returned back home late Saturday evening. Baby, I love you. Thank you for being my cheerleader and support in every way!

Thank you to Daniel Fagot for making my ideas into an actual hardcopy book that is beautiful, powerful, and we tangibly hold in our hands today. Your work went beyond editing, but project managing, and giving me suggestions, real deadlines, pries, etc. ... I loved working with you. You made it fun and you rolled with all of it so well, thank you.

Thank you to all my friends who came by on a rush to make the cover work. We set it all up to have these great pictures taken and it worked! The end result is so wonderful. Thank you for being the models of not just the cover but of someone walking in FREEDOM PEARLS! Debora, Sandra Cris, Jamie, Sylvia, Eirica, and Rebecca you guys don't just add diversity and beauty to these pictures, but depth to illustrate Freedom Pearls Culture. Thanks, girls!

Author Biography

Shaila is a Brazilian-American mother with a heart to shepherd people's hungry hearts well. A lot of her shepherding skills have been first well-tested and tried with her three incredible boys: Samuel (10), Filipe (14), and Nathan (16). They keep her completely dependent on Jesus, and needing more of his love, creativity, and guidance to "mother" well. Her motherly wisdom and experience through the 5-week journey of Freedom Pearls Around the Table comes first and foremost from the wonderful women who mothered her. He mother and grandmothers have been amazing women in the Kingdom and influenced their homes and communities with grace, love, truth, and strength.

Photo by Christian Jacques

Above all, knowing who she is as a daughter of the King and walking confidently in His love even on a "bad day" has made her who she is. Learning to endure pain with joy and be the change she longs to see has made a world of a difference and has been her personal walk with Jesus daily. Shifting atmospheres and bringing heaven into regular realms of daily life is one of her favorite things to do…starting with the heart!

Freedom Pearls Around the Table   Shaila Kerr

All photos by MONTERIO PHOTOGRAPHY unless otherwise specified

CPSIA information can be obtained
at www.ICGtesting.com
Printed in the USA
BVHW020915110520
578317BV00002B/2